STICK WITH IT

Portable Press

An imprint of Printers Row Publishing Group

P.O. Box 1117, Ashland, OR 97520

www.bathroomreader.com

e-mail: mail@bathroomreader.com

Printers Row Publishing Group is a division of Readerlink Distribution Services, LLC.

The Portable Press name and logo is a trademark of Readerlink Distribution Services, LLC.

All correspondence concerning the content of this book should be addressed to Portable Press, Editorial Department, at the above address.

Quotes collected and curated by Hannah L. Bingham

Illustrated and designed by Pete Whitehead

Portable Press would like to thank the following people whose advice and assistance made this book possible:

Gordon Javna	**Jay Newman**	**Rusty von Dyl**
Kim T. Griswell	**Melinda Allman**	**Jonathan Lopes**
Trina Janssen	**Jennifer Magee**	**Aaron Guzman**
Brian Boone	**Peter Norton**	

ISBN: 978-1-62686-475-7

Printed in China

First Printing

20 19 18 17 16   1 2 3 4 5

STICK
WITH IT

QUIRKY SUCCESS QUOTES
THAT STICK
IN YOUR MEMORY...
AND ON YOUR STUFF.

**PORTABLE
PRESS**

You
don't
have
TO BE GREAT
to start,
but you
have to
START
to be great.

ZIG ZIGLAR

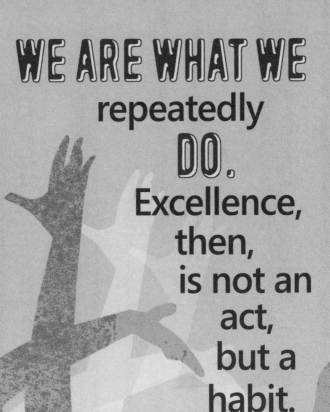

WE ARE WHAT WE
repeatedly
DO.
Excellence,
then,
is not an
act,
but a
habit.

Aristotle

You're
never
a loser
until
you
quit
trying.

Mike Ditka

THE MOST COURAGEOUS
ACT IS STILL
TO
think
for
yourself.

Coco Chanel

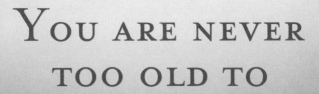

YOU ARE NEVER TOO OLD TO

set another goal
or to

DREAM

a new dream.

———

C. S. Lewis

OPPORTUNITY

IS MISSED BY MOST PEOPLE BECAUSE IT IS DRESSED IN OVERALLS AND

LOOKS LIKE WORK.

Thomas A. Edison

Forget about the fast lane.

If you really want to fly, just

HARNESS YOUR

power to your

PASSION.

Oprah

TRY TO **BE** LIKE THE TURTLE, **AT EASE** IN YOUR OWN SHELL.

BILL COPELAND

NEVER FOLLOW

SOMEONE ELSE'S PATH

UNLESS YOU'RE LOST IN

THE WOODS AND YOU SEE A PATH,

THEN, BY ALL MEANS, YOU

SHOULD FOLLOW THAT.

—ELLEN DEGENERES

IF YOU THINK YOU ARE
TOO SMALL TO
MAKE A
DIFFERENCE
TRY
SLEEPING
WITH A
MOSQUITO.
DALAI LAMA

Life is a shipwreck but we must not forget to

SING

in the lifeboats.

Voltaire

Never give up,
for that is
just the place
and time that
THE TIDE WILL TURN.

Harriet Beecher Stowe

EVEN IF **YOU ARE ON THE RIGHT TRACK,** YOU'LL GET RUN OVER IF YOU JUST SIT THERE.

NEVER GIVE UP

*on something
that you
can't go a
day without
thinking about.*

Winston Churchill

My therapist told me the way to **ACHIEVE TRUE INNER PEACE** *is to finish what I start.*

So far I've finished two bags of M&Ms and a chocolate cake. I feel better already.

Dave Barry

Always **BE** a first-rate version of **YOURSELF,** instead of a second-rate version of somebody else.

Judy Garland

If you cannot **do great things,** do small things in a great way.

Napolean Hill

To
BE
tested
is good.
The
CHALLENGED
life may
be the
best
therapist

Gail Sheehy

DON'T WORRY

about the world coming
to and end today.

It's already tomorrow
in Australia.

Charles Schulz

Strive
not
TO BE A SUCCESS,
but
rather to
BE OF VALUE.

Albert
Einstein

If you're feeling low,
DON'T DESPAIR.
The sun has a sinking spell
every night,
but it comes
back up
every morning.
Dolly Parton

You can never cross
the ocean until you

HAVE

the

COURAGE

to lose sight of the shore.

Christopher Columbus

'May the Force
be with you'
is charming but
it's not important.
What's important
is that you
BECOME THE FORCE
for yourself
and perhaps
for other people.

Harrison Ford

Always concentrate on how far you have come, rather than how far you have left to go.

Heidi Johnson

BIG SHOTS

are only little shots who

KEEP SHOOTING.

Christopher Morley

Give a girl the right
shoes, and she can

CONQUER
THE WORLD.

Marilyn Monroe

As soon as you

TRUST
YOURSELF,

you will know
how to live.

GOETHE

Life's like a movie,
WRITE YOUR OWN ENDING.
Keep believing, keep pretending.

Jim Henson

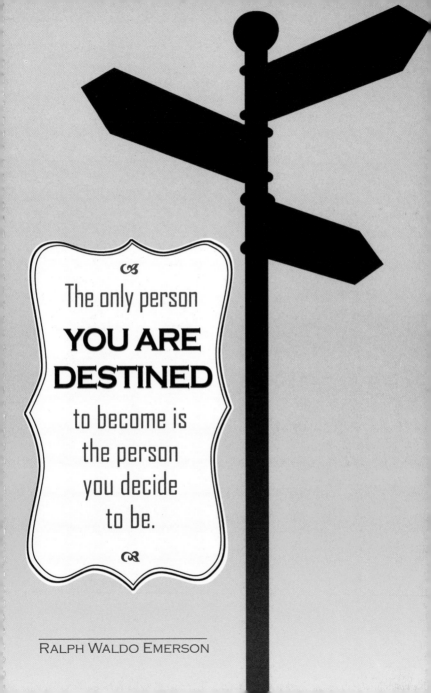

WE CAN EASILY

FORGIVE

A CHILD WHO IS AFRAID
OF THE DARK;
THE REAL TRAGEDY
OF LIFE IS WHEN MEN
ARE AFRAID OF
THE LIGHT.

PLATO

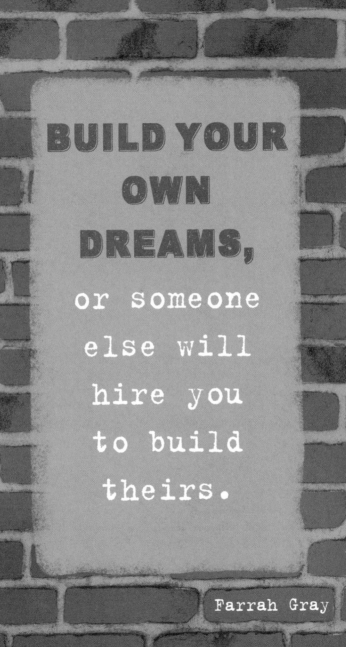

BUILD YOUR OWN DREAMS, or someone else will hire you to build theirs.

Farrah Gray

Only those who will **RISK GOING TOO FAR** can possibly find out how far one can go.

T.S. Eliot

Your time is limited, so **don't waste** it living someone else's **life**.

Steve Jobs

IF YOU WANT

TO MAKE

YOUR

DREAMS COME TRUE,

THE FIRST THING
YOU HAVE TO DO IS

WAKE UP.

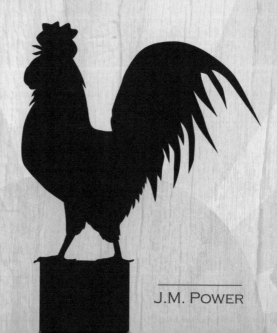

J.M. POWER

Become so wrapped up in something you

FORGET TO BE AFRAID.

Lady Bird Johnson

You must be the
CHANGE
you wish to see in
THE WORLD.

Mahatma Gandhi

Those who dance are considered insane by those that don't hear the music.

George Carlin

EITHER WRITE
SOMETHING WORTH
READING OR

DO SOMETHING

WORTH WRITING.

BENJAMIN FRANKLIN

You
can
only live
once,
but if you
do it right,
once is
enough.

Mae West

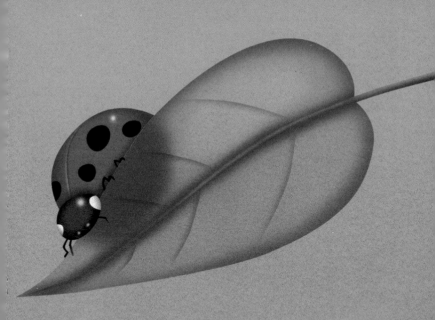

Enjoy the little things

in life because one day
you'll look back and realize
they were the big things.

———————

Kurt Vonnegut

Whether you think

YOU CAN

or you think you can't,

you're right.

Henry Ford

You can take no credit
for beauty at 16. But if

YOU ARE BEAUTIFUL

at 60, it will be
your soul's own doing.

Marie Stopes

LIFE IS
DEEP AND
SIMPLE,
AND WHAT OUR
SOCIETY GIVES US
IS SHALLOW AND
COMPLICATED.

MR. ROGERS

IF YOU'RE GOING THROUGH HELL KEEP GOING

WINSTON CHURCHILL

DREAM OF A BETTER TOMORROW,

WHERE CHICKENS CAN CROSS THE ROAD AND NOT BE QUESTIONED ABOUT THEIR MOTIVES.

UNKNOWN

WE **DON'T STOP PLAYING**
BECAUSE WE GROW OLD;
WE GROW OLD BECAUSE
WE STOP PLAYING.

GEORGE BERNARD SHAW

You can't
BE BRAVE
if you've only had
wonderful things
happen to you.

Mary Tyler Moore

Life is like riding a bicycle.
To keep your balance,
you must

KEEP MOVING.

Albert Einstein

WE ARE WHAT WE
PRETEND TO BE, SO WE MUST
BE CAREFUL
ABOUT WHAT WE
PRETEND TO BE.

KURT VONNEGUT

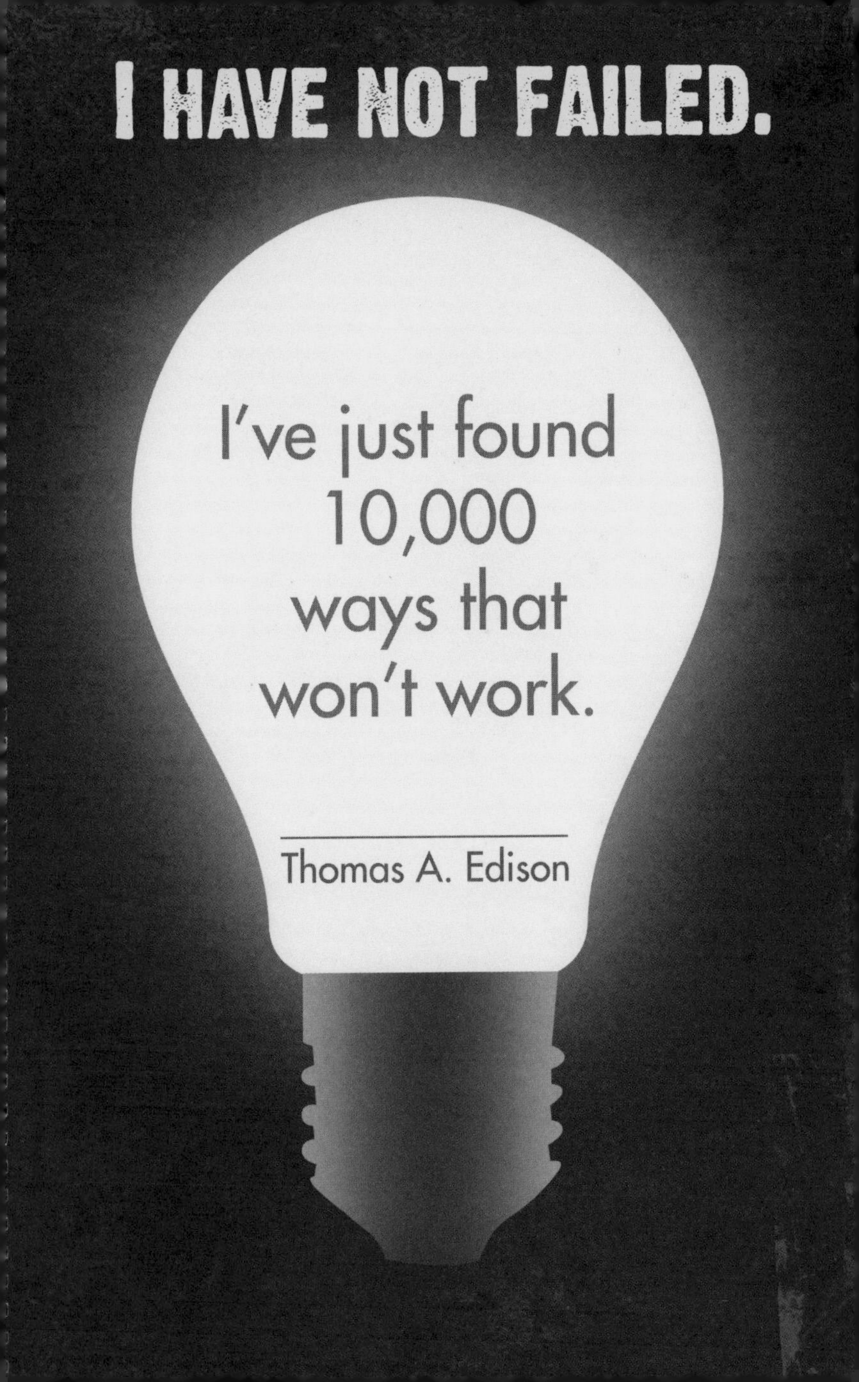
I HAVE NOT FAILED.
I've just found 10,000 ways that won't work.
Thomas A. Edison

NEWS

Don't
PAY
ATTENTION
to bad reviews.
Today's newspaper
is tomorrow's
toilet paper.

Jack Warner

NEVER DOUBT THAT A
SMALL GROUP OF THOUGHTFUL,
COMMITTED CITIZENS CAN
**CHANGE THE
WORLD.**
INDEED, IT IS THE ONLY
THING THAT EVER HAS.

MARGARET MEAD

Life's
hard.
It's even
harder when you're stupid.

John Wayne

You cannot
find peace
by avoiding life.

Virginia Woolf

Life can only be understood backwards; but it must be lived forwards.

Søren Kierkegaard

*Imperfection
is beauty,
madness is genius,
and it's better to*

BE
ABSOLUTELY
RIDICULOUS

*than absolutely
boring.*

Marilyn Monroe

We are all
in the gutter,
but some of us are

looking
at the stars.

Oscar Wilde

WANTING TO **be**
SOMEONE ELSE
IS A WASTE OF
who you are.

KURT COBAIN

It took me quite
a long time to

develop
a voice,

and now that
I have it, I am
not going to
be silent.

Madeleine Albright

Strong people
DON'T PUT OTHERS DOWN.

They lift them up.

Michael P. Watson

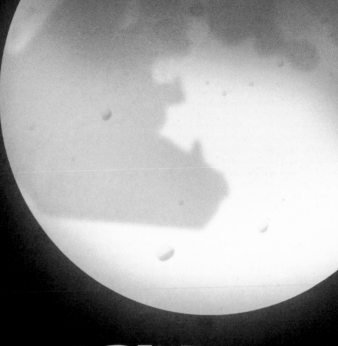

DON'T
tell me the sky's the
LIMIT
when there are footprints
on the moon.

Paul Brandt

Whatever
you
are,
BE
a
GOOD
one.

Abraham Lincoln

Isn't it nice to think that

TOMORROW IS A NEW DAY

with no mistakes in it yet?

———————

L.M. Montgomery

Fairy tales are more than true:
not because they tell us that
dragons exist, but because
they tell us that

DRAGONS CAN
BE BEATEN.

— Neil Gaiman

The future belongs to
those who
BELIEVE IN
the beauty of their
DREAMS.

Eleanor Roosevelt

YOU
NEVER
FAIL
UNTIL
YOU
STOP
TRYING.

ALBERT EINSTEIN

WE ARE JUST AN ADVANCED BREED OF MONKEYS ON A MINOR PLANET OF A VERY AVERAGE STAR. BUT WE CAN UNDERSTAND THE UNIVERSE. THAT MAKES US SOMETHING VERY **SPECIAL**.

STEPHEN HAWKING

IT IS NEVER TOO LATE

to be what you
might have been.

George Eliot

LIFE IS

THE

ART

OF DRAWING

WITHOUT

AN ERASER.

JOHN W. GARDNER

We have to
DARE TO BE
ourselves, however
frightening or
STRANGE
that self may
prove to be.

May Sarton

OPPORTUNITY DOES NOT KNOCK,

IT PRESENTS ITSELF
WHEN YOU BEAT DOWN THE DOOR.

KYLE CHANDLER

Find something
you are
passionate
about and
**KEEP TREMENDOUSLY
INTERESTED**
in it.

JULIA CHILD

The reason birds
can fly and
we can't is simply
because they have
perfect faith, for to

have faith

is to have wings.

J.M. Barrie

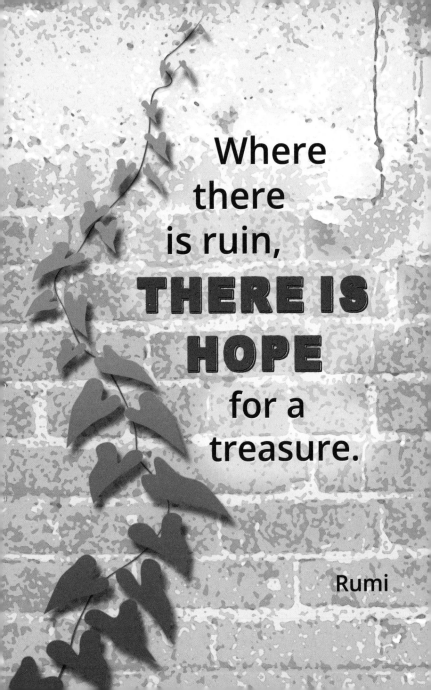

Where
there
is ruin,
**THERE IS
HOPE**
for a
treasure.

Rumi

Why are you
trying so
hard to fit in
when you
were born to
STAND OUT?

_____

Ian Wallace

Around here, we don't look backwards for very long. We **KEEP MOVING FORWARD**, opening up new doors and doing new things, because we're curious... ...and curiosity keeps leading us down new paths.

Walt Disney Company

SOME PEOPLE
FEEL
THE RAIN,
OTHERS JUST GET WET.

BOB MARLEY

Always
DO YOUR BEST.
What you
plant now,
you will
harvest
later.

OG MANDINO

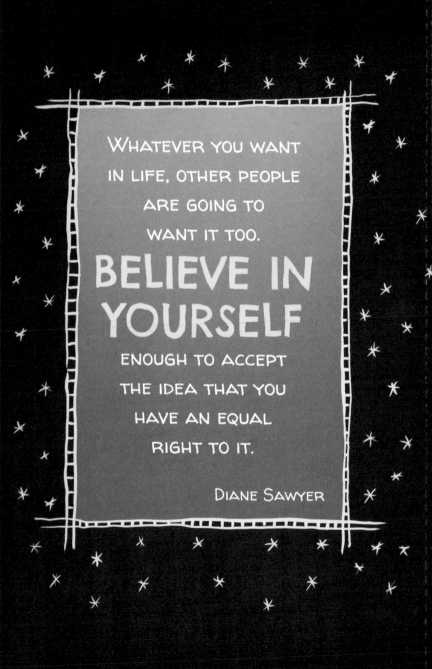

WHATEVER YOU WANT
IN LIFE, OTHER PEOPLE
ARE GOING TO
WANT IT TOO.

BELIEVE IN
YOURSELF

ENOUGH TO ACCEPT
THE IDEA THAT YOU
HAVE AN EQUAL
RIGHT TO IT.

DIANE SAWYER

Without deviation from the norm, **PROGRESS IS** not **POSSIBLE.**

Frank Zappa

When
I was a child
my mother said
to me, "If you
BECOME
a soldier, you'll be a
general. If you
become a monk,
you'll be the pope."
Instead I became
a painter and
wound up
as Picasso.

Pablo Picasso

IF YOU WANT TO
LIVE A HAPPY LIFE,
TIE IT TO A GOAL.
NOT TO PEOPLE
OR THINGS.

ALBERT EINSTEIN

When the power of love overcomes the love of power, the world will **know peace.**

Jimi Hendrix

And above all,
watch with glittering eyes
the whole world around you
because the greatest secrets
are always hidden in the most
unlikely places. Those who don't

BELIEVE IN MAGIC

will never find it.

Roald Dahl

As soon are
you're born,
you start dying,
so you might as well

HAVE A GOOD

TIME.

Cake

BE
YOURSELF.

Everyone else is

already taken.

Oscar Wilde

If you
LOVE LIFE,
don't waste
time.
For time
is what
life is made
up of.

Bruce Lee

Have the courage to
FOLLOW YOUR HEART
and intuition.
They somehow
know what you
truly want to
become.

STEVE JOBS

NOT ALL THOSE WHO

WANDER

ARE LOST.

J.R.R. TOLKIEN

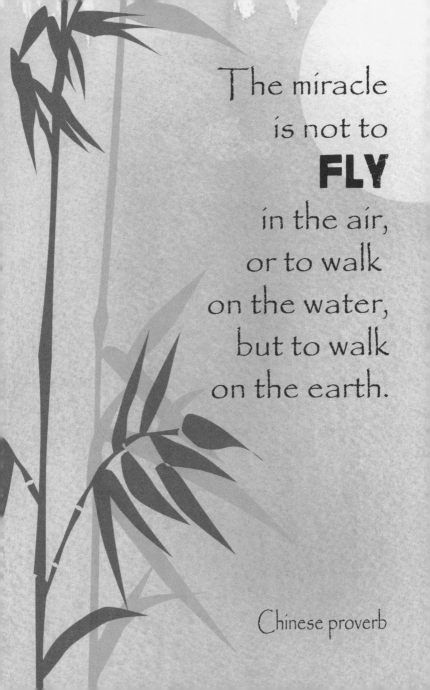

The miracle
is not to
FLY
in the air,
or to walk
on the water,
but to walk
on the earth.

Chinese proverb

TO THINE
OWN SELF
BE TRUE.

WILLIAM SHAKESPEARE

You must
BE PREPARED
to work always
without applause.

Ernest Hemingway

If you don't like being a doormat then

GET OFF THE FLOOR.

Al Anon

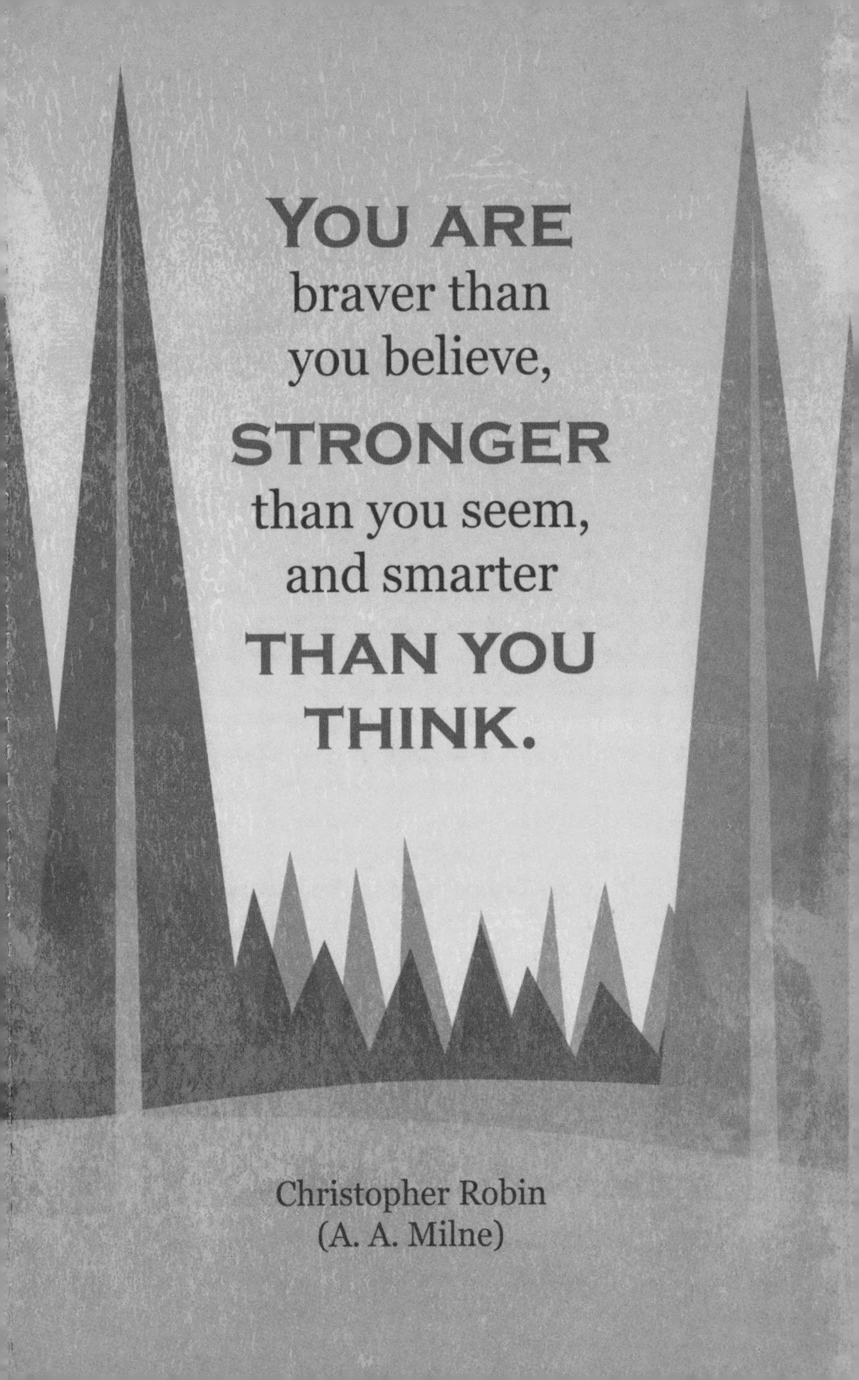
YOU ARE
braver than
you believe,
STRONGER
than you seem,
and smarter
THAN YOU
THINK.
Christopher Robin
(A. A. Milne)

Man can **LEARN** nothing unless he proceeds from the known to **THE UNKNOWN.**

Claude Bernard

Men who try to
DO SOMETHING
and fail
are infinitely better
than those who
try to do
nothing and
succeed.

LLOYD JONES

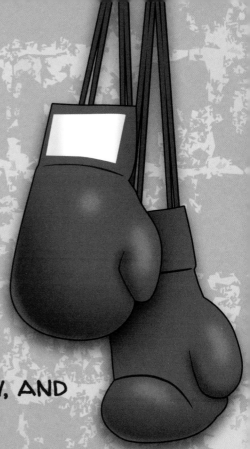

DON'T QUIT.
SUFFER NOW, AND
LIVE
THE REST OF
YOUR LIFE
AS A CHAMPION.

MUHAMMAD ALI

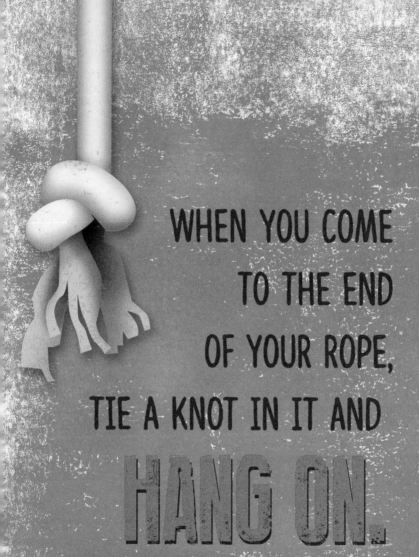

WHEN YOU COME
TO THE END
OF YOUR ROPE,
TIE A KNOT IN IT AND
HANG ON.

THOMAS JEFFERSON

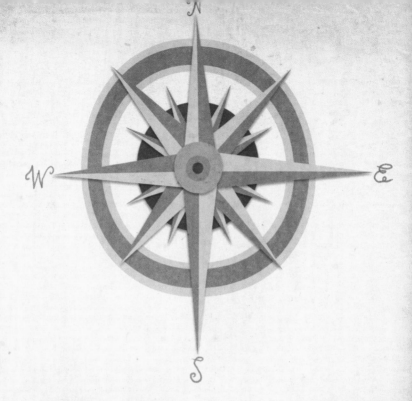

THERE ARE NO SHORTCUTS

to any place worth going.

Beverly Sills

ADMIT ONE

23456603456

23456603456

Life is
a ticket to
**THE GREATEST
SHOW**
on Earth.

Martin H. Fischer

HAPPINESS is not something ready-made. It **COMES FROM** your own **ACTIONS.**

Dalai Lama

You can't wait for inspiration. You have to **GO AFTER IT** with a club.

Jack London

AS SOON AS YOU

TRUST YOURSELF

YOU WILL KNOW
HOW TO LIVE.

Johann Wolfgang Von Goethe

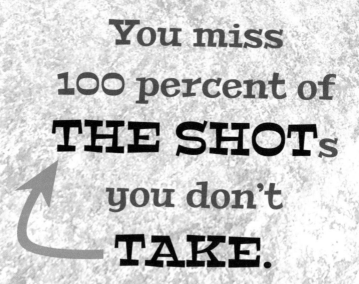

You miss
100 percent of
THE SHOTs
you don't
TAKE.

Wayne Gretzky

What MAKEs night within
us may leave STARS.

Victor Hugo

USE
WHAT
TALENT
YOU POSSESS:
THE WOODS WOULD
BE VERY SILENT IF
NO BIRDS SANG
EXCEPT THOSE
THAT SANG
BEST.

HENRY VAN DYKE

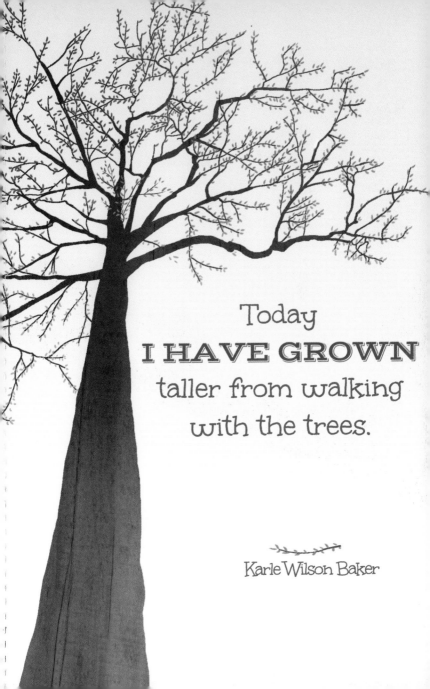

Today
I HAVE GROWN
taller from walking
with the trees.

Karle Wilson Baker

With perseverance, the snail
REACHed THE ARK.

Charles Spurgeon

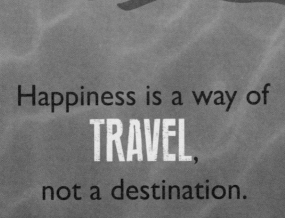

Happiness is a way of
TRAVEL,
not a destination.

Roy L. Goodman

DO SOMETHING WONDERFUL,

PEOPLE MAY IMITATE IT.

ALBERT SCHWEITZER

EVEN THE GREATEST

WAS ONCE A BEGINNER.

DON'T BE AFRAID

TO TAKE THAT

FIRST STEP.

UNKNOWN

I am not here to
change the world.
I AM CHANGING THE WORLD
because I am here.

Lisa Wilson

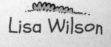

If at first
YOU don't SUCCEED,
find out if
the loser gets
anything.

William Lyon Phelps

You always
Pass
Failure
on the
Way to
Success.

Mickey Rooney

Don't wait around for
other people to
BE HAPPY
for you.
Any happiness
you get
you've got to
make yourself.

...Alice Walker

Whatever you do,
BE DIFFERENT.
If you're different,
you will
STAND OUT.

Anita Roddick

I **DON'T REGRET**
the things I've
done, I regret the
things I didn't do
when I had the chance.

———

Unknown

Before you can
THINK
out of the box,
you have to start
with a box.

Twyla Tharp

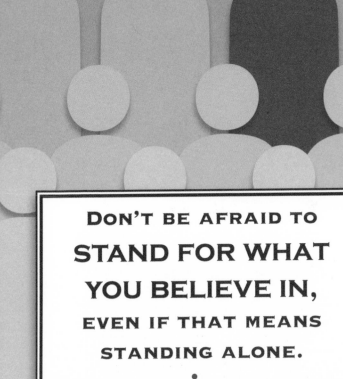

DON'T BE AFRAID TO STAND FOR WHAT YOU BELIEVE IN, EVEN IF THAT MEANS STANDING ALONE.

UNKNOWN

I HONESTLY THINK
IT IS BETTER TO
BE A FAILURE AT
SOMETHING YOU
LOVE THAN
TO BE A SUCCESS
AT SOMETHING YOU
HATE.

GEORGE BURNS

Why not
**GO OUT ON
A LIMB**?
That's where the fruit is.

———————

Mark Twain

PERSEVERANCE IS FAILING 19 times and succeeding the 20th.

Julie Andrews

Nobody ever wrote down a plan to be broke, fat, lazy, or stupid. Those things are what happen when you don't **HAVE A PLAN.**

Larry Winget

NEVER FEAR shadows.
They simply mean
there's a light
shining somewhere
nearby.

Ruth E. Renkel

Choose a job you
LOVE,
and you will
never have
TO WORK
a day in your life.

Confucius

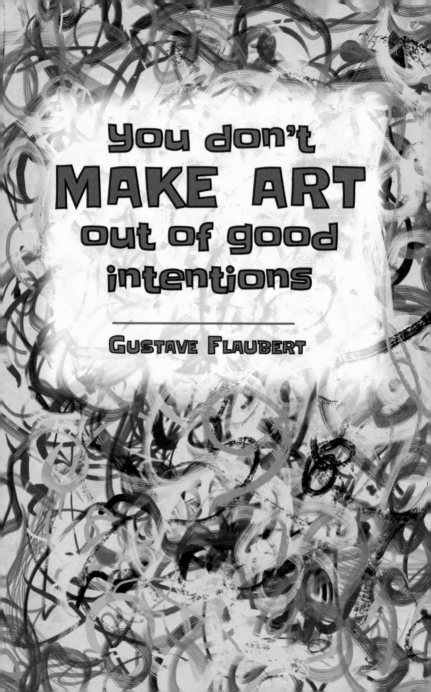

You don't
MAKE ART
out of good
intentions

GUSTAVE FLAUBERT

Everything you need to

BE GREAT

is already inside you.
Stop waiting for
someone or
something to light
your fire.
YOU have the match.

———

Darren Hardy

To succeed **IN LIFE YOU NEED** three things: a wishbone, **A BACKBONE,** and a funny bone.

Reba McEntire

STUFF YOUR EYES WITH WONDER,
**LIVE AS IF YOU'D DROP DEAD
IN TEN SECONDS.**

RAY BRADBURY

What is the point
of being alive if you
don't at least try to
**DO SOMETHING
REMARKABLE?**

John Green

To be successful you must
**ACCEPT
ALL
CHALLENGES**
that come your way.

You can't just accept
the ones you like.

Mike Gafka

Even the smallest person can CHANGE the course of THE FUTURE.

J.R.R. Tolkien

YOU ARE SUCCESSFUL THE MOMENT YOU START MOVING TOWARD A WORTHWHILE GOAL.

CHARLES CARLSON

When you are living the best version of yourself, you **INSPIRE OTHERS** to live the best versions of themselves.

Steve Maraboli

When I
LET GO
of what
I am,
I become
what I
might be.

Lao Tzu

NEVER RETREAT.
Never explain.
Get it done and let them howl.

Benjamin Jowett

I always wanted
to BE SOMEBODY.
Now I realize
I should
have been
more specific.

Lily Tomlin

YOU ARE NEVER TOO OLD TO set another goal or to DREAM a new dream

SUCCEED

BE AT EASE

MAKE A DIFFERENCE

WE ARE WHAT WE DO

BIG SHOTS are only little shots who KEEP SHOOTING.

HARNESS YOUR PASSION

OPPORTUNITY IS MISSED BY MOST PEOPLE BECAUSE IT IS DRESSED IN OVERALLS AND LOOKS LIKE WORK.

TO BE GREAT, START

You're never a loser until you quit trying

NEVER GIVE UP

DON'T WORRY about the world coming to and end today. It's already tomorrow in Australia.

DON'T DESPAIR

If you cannot **do great things,** do small things in a great way

ACHIEVE TRUE INNER PEACE

YOU ARE ON THE RIGHT TRACK

THE TIDE WILL TURN

SING

The **CHALLENGED** life may be the best therapist

DON'T WASTE LIFE

TRUST

Always
Concentrate on how far you have come rather than how far you have left to go.

BUILD YOUR OWN DREAMS, or someone else will hire you to build theirs.

CONQUER

Life's like a movie. **WRITE YOUR OWN ENDING.** *Keep believing, keep pretending.*

DESTINY

HAVE COURAGE

FORGIVE

BECOME THE FORCE

RISK

think for yourself

BE YOURSELF

Whether you think YOU CAN or you think you can't, you're right

PROGRESS

You can only live once, but if you do it right, once is enough.

GO AFTER IT

LOVE LIFE

DON'T BE AFRAID

YOU ARE WORTHWHILE

LEARN THE UNKNOWN

IF YOU WANT **TO MAKE** YOUR **DREAMS COME TRUE,** THE FIRST THING YOU HAVE TO DO IS **WAKE UP.**

FORGET TO BE AFRAID.

You must be the **CHANGE** you wish to see in **THE WORLD**

HEAR THE MUSIC

YOU ARE BEAUTIFUL

LIFE IS SIMPLE

DO SOMETHING

Enjoy the little things

KEEP GOING

THINK BIG

LIFE can only be understood backwards; but it **MUST BE LIVED** forwards.

PAY ATTENTION

DON'T STOP PLAYING

Life's harder when you're stupid

BE CAREFUL

Life is like riding a bicycle. To keep your balance, you must **KEEP MOVING.**

find peace

CHANGE THE WORLD

BE BRAVE

I HAVE NOT FAILED

IT IS NEVER TOO LATE

DRAGONS
CAN BE
BEATEN

DARE TO BE STRANGE

DON'T
LIMIT

Strong
people
DON'T PUT
OTHERS DOWN.
They lift
them up.

BE
GOOD

BE
ABSOLUTELY
RIDICULOUS

develop a voice

be who
you are

BELIEVE IN DREAMS

LIFE IS ART

THERE IS HOPE

TOMORROW IS A NEW DAY

BELIEVE IN MAGIC

KEEP INTERESTED

OPPORTUNITY DOES NOT KNOCK, IT PRESENTS ITSELF WHEN YOU BEAT DOWN THE DOOR.

If you don't like being a doormat then **GET OFF THE FLOOR.**

Life is a ticket to **THE GREATEST SHOW** on earth.

have faith

Why are you trying so hard to fit in when you were born to **STAND OUT**

KEEP MOVING FORWARD

LIVE A HAPPY LIFE

Always DO YOUR BEST. What you plant now, you will harvest later.

SOME PEOPLE FEEL THE RAIN, OTHERS JUST GET WET.

know peace

Believe in yourself

FOLLOW YOUR HEART.

FLY

HAVE A GOOD TIME

You must **BE PREPARED** to work always without applause

I always wanted to BE SOMEBODY. Now I realize I should have been more specific.

WANDER

YOU ARE STRONGER THAN YOU THINK

BE TRUE

GO AFTER IT

DO SOMETHING

LIKE YOURSELF

LIVE AS A CHAMPION

THERE ARE NO SHORTCUTS to any place worth going